Panda Bakes a Cake

Peter Brownlow

It was a beautiful morning and Panda decided that today was the day she would bake a cake.

She got some butter, flour and eggs then mixed them together in a bowl.

She poured the mixture into a baking tin and put it in the oven.

Then she waited for the cake to bake.

When the cake was ready she took it out of the oven, decorated it then put it near the kitchen window.

She washed up and cleared everything away, neat and tidy.

Feeling a bit tired, she had a snooze in her rocking chair.

When she woke up, she found that the cake had gone.

She looked in the cupboard. It wasn't there.

She looked in the pantry. It wasn't there.

Where could it be? Surely she hadn't dreamed about making a cake.

No matter. She would just have to make another one.

When the cake was ready she took it out of the oven, decorated it then put it near the kitchen window.

She washed up and cleared everything away, neat and tidy.

This made her very tired, so she had a snooze on her favourite bed.

When she woke up, she found that the cake had gone.

She looked in the cake tin. It wasn't there.

She looked in the dining room. It wasn't there.

She even looked under the table. But why would it be there?

She couldn't have dreamed about making another cake. Could she?

Panda was starting to think something was not right here.

And looking outside she saw the answer.

Her two baby pandas had eaten both the cakes.

And now they were not feeling very well.

Panda was very cross with the two babies, who were very sorry they ate all the cakes.

It was a birthday cake for you both. You have ruined the surprise.

What am I going to do with you two?

The two baby pandas were sent straight to bed.

Without any supper. Not that they could eat another thing anyway.

Panda made one more cake.

But this one was just for her.

Peter lives on the edge of the West Pennine moors with his wife Debbie and dog Rosie. He has written other children's books including The First Lamb, The First Frog, The Silent Wolf & The Lost Rabbit.

Printed in Great Britain
by Amazon